# THE POWER OF STORY

A Burst of Inspiration to Write and Publish Your Book

**Best-Selling Author**

**Denita Austin**

# A BURST OF INSPIRATION TO WRITE AND PUBLISH YOUR BOOK

**BEST-SELLING AUTHOR**

**DENITA AUSTIN**

**Austin Ink Studio**

**Los Angeles, CA**

# DEDICATION

I dedicate this book to those who need a boost of inspiration to share their story with the world. You may not know how important your story is or how you can inspire others just by believing in what you have to share.

Embrace Your Story – Write Your Story – Publish Your Story

Let the world learn more about you . . .

# THE FLOW OF THIS BOOK

In this unique book, not only will you get inspired to share your story with the world, but I will also walk you through the thought process of it all. You will learn how to begin your writing journey by using your personal story, and the importance of tapping into your memory bank to unlock your extraordinary life experiences. In order to unleash the power of your story from within, one must learn the main challenges that keep us from sharing our story. It's all about learning how to push past these challenges in order to succeed on your writing journey. As you read this book and learn more about yourself, remember you are not alone and we are diving into this writing journey together.

*EMBRACE YOUR STORY – WRITE YOUR STORY*
PUBLISH YOUR STORY

# Table of Contents

*EMBRACE YOUR STORY – WRITE YOUR STORY*

PUBLISH YOUR STORY

# Introduction

Welcome to the Power of Story and the beauty of *Writing Your Journey*! I am super excited that you have decided to dive into a new world of writing, a new world of storytelling, and a new approach to sharing your story with the world. In this uniquely created book, I am not only going to share quite a few things that I've learned on my writing journey, but I will also share a few golden nuggets on how to get there the easy way without all the stress. I absolutely enjoy sharing my own personal experiences, special places that I've traveled, and how to document and capture special moments in your life.

I created the Write Your Journey programs to inspire others to share their story with the world through writing and publishing their book. Not only is it a program, workshop, online course, and even a book, but it's also a community of people around the globe who wish to share their story with passion, raw emotion, and confidence.

Why is sharing your story important? Well, we are all unique individuals. You are unique simply because there's only one you. That means we all—and yes, that includes you—have a unique story to share. And the truth is, no one can tell your story better than you can.

It doesn't matter if the story is about great times in your life, tears of joy or sadness. Some of the worst experiences in our lives created who we are today, and they are well worth telling. Writing your story down allows you to share special memories with others, inspire, motivate, encourage, and transform the lives of others through what you have experienced and learned. Knowledge is power, and exposure can change one's life.

I inspire you to take the time to write, photograph, record, and capture your life experiences. Each moment is special in your life, and you shouldn't take it for granted. By doing this, not only are you inspiring others to do the same, but you're also building your confidence and self-esteem without realizing it.

Who am I to teach you how to do this? If you are not familiar with my work, let me introduce myself. My name is Denita Austin, and I am a best-selling author, lover of all things art, passionate storyteller, and publisher. I am also a certified yoga teacher of thirteen years, and I absolutely love what I do. I love people, I love stories, and I love getting to know people for who they really are.

Sharing your whole story, the good and the bad, helps people learn more about you and why you have made the choices you have made in life. It also helps you understand yourself better and be less judgmental of others, when you realize that maybe they have faced hard choices you don't fully understand. Most importantly, what you share can give people hope in seemingly hopeless situations, inspiration to keep trying and keep going, priceless knowledge and wisdom, and maybe even an escape from the stress of life—depending on what you decide to share. Plus, you can feel a sense of accomplishment and purpose from doing so.

In the end, it is up to you whether you share what you have written or not. But I encourage you to share your story with the world. Even if you don't formally publish it, you can invite friends over for story time, or create a private meetup group to share, bond, and connect. This type of sharing connects us all more deeply!

Before you grab your coffee, tea, or favorite beverage to begin this book, I encourage you to download my free Write Your Journey template on my website to get you started on your writing journey. It will help you tap into your memory bank to grab a memorable story to share. Let's get started!

**YOUR TIME IS NOW**

# Chapter 1
# Boost Of Inspiration

The first thing I would like you to do is write down ten things you love about yourself, using the template you printed. I know you're probably asking, why am I writing this down? How does this relate to writing your journey, and why is this even important? When I first started writing and journaling, I didn't have any confidence, and my self-esteem was super low. I needed something to believe in. I needed a boost of inspiration, and I needed a push to get the work done that was required. Before we can do anything physically, we must be strong and inspired mentally. This is why I am asking you to write down ten things you love about yourself. I want you to feel amazing when you start your writing journey. I want you to believe in yourself and your story. I want you to understand how important your story is and how it can inspire and transform lives. We spend so much time focusing on other people that we forget about ourselves. Let me ask you a question: do you really know what self-love is? Well, you are about to tell me when you write down ten things you love about yourself. Once you do that, I want you to put it someplace where you can look at it every single day, because while you're on this writing journey, you need to be reminded of those ten things. This will serve the purpose of inspiring, motivating, and pushing you to reach your writing goals, and this will also help you complete your book if you choose to do so.

When I first decided to share my story, I didn't have anyone to hold me by the hand and help me focus and believe in my story. Some of us are pretty solid in this area, self-assured and motivated, which is great, but there are a few others, such as myself at the time, that need a little bit more of a push. I also needed to know that my story was important and that it could inspire others, so this is exactly why I'm telling you to be open and try something new. Anyone can write a story, but it's a matter of being connected to your story, really feeling the emotion behind it and the passion behind it all. If you're going to tell a story, I say put every single ounce of energy you have into it. Don't just write the story to write it, share it with passion. I want you to know that this is supposed to be fun, so if you have any judgments in your mind, let them go. Any distractions that surround you, remove them from your life and try something different. We create all of these rules in our head, and for what? Where does that get us? Be free within yourself, be free within your story, and believe that whatever you have to say matters. I'm here to help you every single step of the way.

After you write down those ten things on the template that's provided on the website, think about how you feel. Why did you choose those ten things? Are these other people's perspectives of you? Is this truly how you feel about yourself? What is it? This is an opportunity for you to stop and take time for yourself and just focus on you. We all are guilty of being so caught up in our jobs, careers, and responsibilities that we neglect ourselves. Well I'm definitely here to tell you those days are over, so flip the page of your life and tell the story. I don't want you to read this book because it's just another book on your shelf or in your virtual library. I want you to read this book with a writing goal in mind. Do it! Remember, I'm here to share my personal experiences with you and to give guidance and support on your writing journey. You share with me and I will share with you. I want you to know that it was super hard for me to share some of the stories I decided to share so far in books, articles and workshops, but it was the best decision ever.

Now that you've completed your self-love list, let's talk about five memorable experiences in your life, using the template from the website. Think of five of your most memorable experiences, things you think you can write about, and list them on this template. Your story can literally be about any memorable experience. Whether you decide to tell about the best Halloween costume you ever had or the rock band you were part of in your mind but never existed, it doesn't matter. It's your story, so tell it!

I can't stress enough whether your experience was good or bad, you're giving someone hope for the opportunity to experience the same as you. Let's be honest, even your bad moments helped you grow as a person. I'm sure your experiences made you think outside the box and pushed you out of your comfort zone. It made you a stronger person, and you were able to leave that place on a higher frequency from within, right? On your worksheet, it will ask you to list five amazing places you've traveled. Even if you only have one destination in your memory bank, ask yourself what made that experience memorable? If you were sitting with a group of friends, would you share this special story with them? Why is the story close to your heart? If it's a story that you're willing to share with your friends and family and loved ones, it's definitely a story everyone else would want to read as well. Your topic of choice can be anything.

I'm sure you have a story in your back pocket that you are dying to tell someone. Let's see, is it about your first job, is it about becoming a mom for the first time? What about the transformational vacation you took last year? It could be about your first business as an entrepreneur. What about your family history or heritage? It could be a personal story of adoption or possibly your transformation after divorce. What about your personal story of being an introvert? There are so many choices here, and I'm hoping I pushed a button to make you think. Believe it or not, I can relate to the topic of introverts simply because I'm an introvert and I understand that world on every level.

Everyone has a story, even if your story is about your self-love journey and you want to share that you haven't quite figured it out yet or you don't even know what it means but you want to take others on the journey with you to understand it all. Your writing journey is all about sharing what you've learned, what you're going through, how you're overcoming the challenges, and how it's transformed your world for the better. You will be able to use your personal story to write and publish a book in no time. Just take a stand and tap into that memory bank. There is a story that we all are waiting to read. I can't stress it enough: your story is extremely important, and there's only one you, and no one will tell the story better than you, of course. Remember, it's your personal experience, so before diving into chapter 2, I want you to take your time and really dig deep on what you are willing to share with the world. There are so many stories in your life experience box, so which experience changed your life or transformed your way of thinking? Think of something that was monumental. Once you've gotten that down, you have the beginning of your story!

*EMBRACE YOUR STORY – WRITE YOUR STORY*
PUBLISH YOUR STORY

**WHAT STORY ARE YOU LIVING?**

# Chapter 2
# Overcoming the Fear of Sharing Your Story

Yes, it's true, we all are fearful of something. We are so focused on what we are scared of that we don't have any energy left to focus on the solution, and, yes, we all are guilty of it—including me, in this chapter. I want to share with you the challenges and obstacles that keep us from sharing our story with the world and on a smaller scale our loved ones.

First let's examine what it is that we are so afraid of anyway. I mean, really, what's the big deal? Will life really be over if we share something that makes us vulnerable? Who really cares? When you take that stand and decide to own your story and embrace your story, nothing can stop you. That in itself is something to celebrate. It takes courage to do this. It doesn't really matter what someone thinks of it, because you're simply sharing your story for you first.

Yes, I talk a lot about sharing your story with the world to inspire others, but please don't forget that the first reason and number one reason to share your story is to do it for yourself. What do I mean by this? Sharing your experiences is simply for you to overcome the fear of it all. It's for you to let go of your past and to push past the pain of hurt or rise above it all. It could be a story of pain, pleasure, inspiration, or transformation, whichever you choose to share, but just remember that when you're sharing your experiences for yourself first, it will feel like a sense of accomplishment and a special gift to yourself.

Not only are we going to talk about how to push past that fear of sharing your story, but we're also going to talk about how to unleash the power of your story from within. The number one reason for not sharing your personal story is fear of judgment. It's common to get stuck on "no one will read my story" or "I'm not the best writer" or "I don't have a story important enough to tell." I am here to tell you, it's really not about that.

Here is the main thing we need to understand: why we are so afraid of being judged. It could be a worry about not being accepted, possibly being misunderstood, wanting to please everyone, or just wanting to appear a certain way, but if you really take a step back and think about it, who are these people you actually want to be understood by? Who are these people that are important enough to give their opinion of who they think you are? Honestly, it doesn't really matter if you appear a certain way to whomever. It's time for you to live your life on your terms. I'm going to bring this topic up later on in this book when we start discussing the goals of you sharing your story, but for now let's stay focused on you pushing past the fear. By now, I hope you're saying the hell with fear. Who cares about it? I hope you're saying, Denita, I honestly gave Fear the big black boot and I'm ready to move forward.

Then, before you can write your story for the world to read, before you can even consider getting started, you have to really think about the first question to ask yourself, which is, what story will I share with the world, and am I committed to that story? I have to embrace that story, so am I ready to do that? Embracing your story is the first step, and the key to embracing your story is understanding your value and making peace with whatever that story was about. You can't move forward from your story if you haven't embraced it. Now, of course, this would only apply to a story of pain or something that was so catastrophic that you haven't chosen to deal with it. Again, embrace it, make peace with it, and work through it. If you feel as though the story is not ready to be told because you haven't done the inner work to release that story, choose another one to share. Everything takes time.

Now let me share one of my personal stories with you that I'm actually releasing in this book for the very first time. This story is very special to me simply because I was at a vulnerable place in my life, and my world completely crumbled before my eyes. This uncomfortable and life-changing experience molded me into the person I am today, so for that I am grateful, but I didn't think this way at the time of going through it all. I was hesitant to share this with you simply because I thought it was super embarrassing and I didn't want to be judged. I literally felt like I would rather jump off the nearest roof than share the story with you. Sound familiar? But guess what? I learned that it doesn't matter.

I learned that when you decide to share your story and you actually push through it, it actually feels like a complete boulder has been lifted off of your shoulders. Before you read it, I just want to say thank you for giving me the platform to share my story with you, and thank you for embracing it with open arms. Here it is:

> Ever since I was a young child, I've always wanted to live in California. It really didn't matter where, just anywhere in the state. I desired to be near an ocean, near mountains, and near palm trees. I wanted that perfect glowing skin that exudes happiness. I would sit in front of the TV at a young age staring at palm trees and the sunny beaches were just mesmerizing, and to be honest, I just really felt like it was someplace I belonged. Well, guess what? I made it, and it has been quite the journey.
>
> When I first moved to California, I lived in a beautiful beach town which was only a few blocks away from the beach. It was absolutely beautiful. Here's the thing though: even though

it was so beautiful, I was very intimidated at how massive California was. I mean, seriously, you could drive yourself crazy just looking at the map. Needless to say, I became a hermit for a few months before I was able to settle in. My lifestyle started changing slowly, and I honestly didn't know how to handle it. I wasn't able to digest the same foods, my hair texture started changing, and even my skin required more lotion. It's okay, you can laugh, it's funny—well, the skin part, that is. I mean, I really felt like I was on another planet. I had to keep in mind that no matter where you decide to live in the world, every single place is different: culture, food, environment, and perspective. I was beyond excited and ready to dive in despite my fear. I didn't even realize how conservative I was until I moved to California, and every morning it was so sunny that it was impossible not to wear sunglasses. I do believe people think it's a fashion statement in LA, but honestly, for some it may be, but for the most part the sun is so damn bright you can't see a damn thing. But, hey, it's still beautiful, right? If you plan on visiting California, bring some shades or even two pairs, and make sure they are awesome. (This is when you smile.)

Getting to the point before you get bored with my story, within three months my world changed drastically. My three-and-a-half -year relationship came to a screeching halt, and I damn near lost my damn mind. I honestly didn't know what to do since my relationship was my world. This may sound familiar to some ladies, and while we are on this topic, why do we do that— get lost in others, that is, and forget about ourselves? Okay, food for thought, moving on. But that relationship literally was my life, and I put so much work into it and thought that it was for me. I told myself, "Hooray, you did a great job with this relationship. You did everything by the book (well, the book in my head), so it can only be great and lead to marriage and living happily ever after." How about, no, it doesn't end that way. When this relationship ended as soon as I moved to California, I fell into the deepest depression of my life. I had relocated by myself to a state that was just beyond me. I had no family and no close friends and, honestly, not much money. I am from Washington, DC, so that would have been a long trip back. So I ask you, what would you do? If you were in my shoes, what would be your first decision? Would you go back home, or would you stay in a state where you don't know a soul?

I could go into more detail about this, but that's not what this book is about, and trust me, if I did, you would probably cry for days. So I ended up moving to the heart of LA, I mean the very heart of the city. I've never lived in a city in my life. (I will pull the suburban card in a second.) I love the suburbs. Why? you ask. Well, you get to listen to birds chirping instead of fire trucks driving by—should I go on with this? I think you get the point. I didn't move to LA by choice. My personal life began to crumble before me and I had no choice but to move. I lost everything to my name. You name it, I lost it. My business was crumbling because of my depression, my money was beyond low, and I had lost a piece of my heart. I was literally surprised it was still beating at that point. I only knew a handful of people in California, but the handful of people that I did know didn't even offer to help. I actually remember asking one person if I could stay with them until I actually got on my feet, and I received every excuse possible. My friends back home didn't even call to say, "Hey, can we send you some cash?" or "Come back here. It's okay," or even just call to say hello. This was one of the lowest points in my life. I looked for the quickest way out of the situation, to fix it immediately. And remember, this was just three months after I moved to California, the place I had dreamed of all my life.

This is another reason I stress to my clients, friends, and loved ones, take the time to listen to someone's story. Trust me, you will actually meet them for the first time when you listen to their story, even if you've known them for years. Never judge a book by its cover. Read the entire book. Literally! Anyway, back to the story, writing and publishing books full time for myself was a blessing. It was the career I chose after leaving the job I had for a few years with the federal government, and I enjoyed it. I had worked for myself for a complete year already before moving, and things had been going great, until I had to shift gears.

I must say to you that I have experienced more just living in Los Angeles alone than I have my entire life. Let me explain. I have traveled quite a bit. There isn't an island I haven't been to, and there are a few places that I've visited in the UK, but what I'm talking about is a fresh experience of brutal life. Some of us have lost jobs, houses, and even cars. Maybe gone through a divorce or some sort of separation. I had to do the unthinkable and make the most uncomfortable decisions ever. My life in the city was so brutal that I wouldn't wish it on my worst enemy. Now my brutal may be peanuts to some, but, hey, we all have our levels and limitations, and by no means would I ever compare my story to someone else's hardship. We all have our experiences; that's not what this is about.

Let's talk real estate. First off, living in California taught me that it's okay to rent apartments with no kitchens. Yes, you heard me: no kitchens—what the hell. I am still trying to wrap my head around that. I didn't even know that was legal. Here are a few examples: apartment, 350 square feet open space with bathroom, $1,300. I know you're asking, well how do you eat? You eat out, wow . . . Another apartment, 450 square feet, partial kitchen, $1250. Uh, what the hell is a partial kitchen? Oh, this means you will get two cabinets, a mini fridge, and possibly a microwave. Did you catch that? No kitchen sink and no stove. What the hell is going on here? I don't think this would be a problem if you were looking for a tent. I've even learned that developers enjoy remodeling 1960s Motel 6s and remodeling them into studio apartments. Once again, this means a room, bathroom, and kitchenette.

And by the way, I am not bashing California—absolutely not—because California has some amazing places to discover. I'm only sharing my experience of when I first moved to the city, just so you know. All apartments are not as I described above. I was just shocked that this sort of renting existed at all, and let me tell you, when you are on a budget, I guess these are your options. Life is much different now, but this story must be shared. So, needless to say, I ended up living in a shoe box probably the size of someone's walk-in closet back home on the East Coast. I hated every minute of it, but it allowed me to be more active and explore the world a bit more. I guess if I had enjoyed my place too much I would have never left home, and that's easy for me to do considering I'm kind of a home body at heart if I'm comfortable. Since I had the worst place ever to live in California, I explored all of the beautiful things, such as hiking, museums, concerts, horseback riding, you name it. It allowed me to do the things I love. It pushed me to dive into my creativity and happiness. *I believe we are placed in situations to help us grow and become stronger.* If things stay the same or if we are always comfortable we will never really strive or get pushed beyond our limits, and I believe we all need that. I am clearly not the same person I was when I moved to California, and I have to thank my experiences, even if they were brutal and unpleasant.

I spent a year with no sleep simply because of Billy at the dumpster yelling and arguing over trash at 4:00 a.m. every single morning. (And, yes, Billy is a made-up name.) I wasn't sure of the name of this interesting character, and I really don't think that's important. I share this with you simply because people don't truly understand someone's life or what they may be going through, so never assume. *Take the time to listen to someone's story to get to know them better.*

So, let's wrap this up, shall we? The bright side of this experience was simply falling in love with Airbnb. It was my savior. This amazing platform became my best friend in California, due to my unique living conditions. I decided to travel with in the state of California as much as I could my first year living in the city. Let me tell you, that was the best experience I could've ever had, and I would recommend doing this every chance you get. Not only for meeting great hosts, but also for the transformational experiences. I had the pleasure of visiting everything from beautiful cabins and cottages up in the mountains, to Hollywood lofts in the city. I've stayed in Airstreams in the desert, meeting new friends as I woke up to cactuses and fresh warm quiet air. I was so grateful to explore all of these things just because my life wasn't as perfect as I planned it to be at home. None of this was expensive, by the way. Less than a hotel. One day I was sitting in this cute little cabin literally no bigger than a shed. It was just perfect. Four little windows with this beautiful wooden door that would remind you of something in a children's

> story book such as “Little Red Riding Hood.” It had everything you could possibly need, and a comfortable bed with a thousand pillows for comfort. You get the point, right? I figure that if I had been living this perfect life I felt I needed to live, then I wouldn’t have pushed myself to explore all of these unknown places. This unique experience helped me grow as a person, and it allowed me to create material to write and to share these amazing experiences with you, which I love.

If you would’ve asked me to share this story with you two years ago, I would’ve hid under the bed with my blanket, but what would be the point of that, right? So thank you again for allowing me to share my story with you. At this point, can I ask you to do me a small favor? Write three major challenges—or should I say, excuses—that block your writing goals. Once you complete that, write three solutions on how to overcome those challenges and excuses. Usually we have the answers to our questions but we just don’t think about it simply because we are too focused on whatever the challenge may be. Remember, you only get one life. Live it and stop wasting time creating excuses! Write your answers down on the Write Your Journey template that was provided on the website.

*EMBRACE YOUR STORY – WRITE YOUR STORY*
PUBLISH YOUR STORY

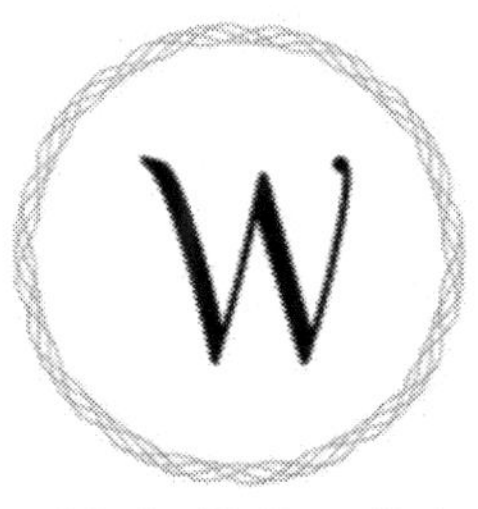

WRITE YOUR JOURNEY

*Life Experiences Published!*

WHAT STORY WILL YOU TELL THE WORLD?

# Chapter 3
# Building Your Support System

You made it to chapter 3. Do you know what that tells me? You are serious and want to move forward with your writing journey. I think you may be jumping on the commitment wagon of accomplishing your writing goals. Good for you! Let's go!

Here's the first question I have for you. Do you have a support system for your writing? You may be asking, well, what do you mean? I'm simply talking about a support system such as a writing mentor or an accountability partner such as a loved one or sibling. What about an online community or focused group? If you do, that is fantastic news. I believe everyone should have some sort of supportive tribe and circle to help them accomplish their goals.

I honestly didn't know how important it was to be part of a community, group, or support circle until I started writing. It doesn't matter if it's online, face-to-face, monthly, weekly, or over the phone. As long as you have a support system, that's all that matters. If you don't have one, I'll give you a few suggestions throughout the rest of the chapter. Grab a notepad to take some notes, or record your notes on your phone, whatever is best for you. I'm assuming you are already doing this, but if not, please start. As I stress in each chapter, don't read this book just to read it; I want you to be inspired to make things happen for yourself. It's about taking that first step.

I recommend finding a group online or in person. Research a few communities in your city/state that can support exactly what you're doing. You could even work with a family member. It doesn't matter who it is. As long as you have someone helping you reach that goal, then you can check this step off your list. It could be a total stranger that will help you on this writing journey. Don't underestimate anyone on your path. The person who could help you become who you want to be could be anybody. Exhaust the possibilities of finding what you need, and keep in mind that you have to take full responsibility for your happiness and accomplishing your goals. It's important to create or join your circle that will help you get to the next level on your journey.

I would like to share with you one of our special groups that we created specifically for creative, ambitious writers, storytellers, and bloggers who wish to share a story. This may be something you're interested in, and if so, this is great news. It's called the **Write Your Journey Ambassador Program**. You're probably asking yourself, what does that even mean—speak English! The Write Your Journey Ambassador Program was designed to help you navigate through your writing challenges with like-minded individuals, and it's super easy to join just like any other group. Everyone in the group is tackling their writing challenges and problems together. The program will allow you to discuss topics of interest, lean on each other, and give advice, share connections, and collaborate with each other, if appropriate. So if you are a creative writer, storyteller, or blogger, or just someone who wishes to share their personal story, this may be for you—you never know. Just as an example of who might benefit from this type of program and workshop, I recommend that writers who may need help in the beginning stages of sharing their story, join a writing group, mastermind, or club. But before joining, think about what your needs are so you can get the best out of your investment. For example, the Write Your Journey Program perks feature goal setting meetings, group coaching calls, homework worksheets, and templates for writing and publishing goals. We also have live workshops and dinners, and phenomenal yearly retreats, just to name a few. It's basically a community built around your writing needs. You could be interested in writing a blog, a short story, or a novel, or writing about your personal stories and experiences. It may even be your travel story. It just depends on your mood or focus in this chapter of your life that you wish to express and share.

Whatever you decide to do or whatever group you join, make sure it's something that supports your goal. One of the greatest benefits of joining a club, mastermind or having a circle of supporters is that you will start to think bigger. Others will push you harder, and we all need that. Wouldn't you agree? Let's be honest: when you're comfortable, you don't push as hard, right? Joining a group that will hold you accountable and motivate you is all about plugging into something bigger than yourself. It's about helping you stretch beyond your boundaries, and when you're surrounded by amazing people, you end up doing amazing things. Everyone is unique in their own special way. Your skillset, experience, and connections will allow you to create a new chapter in your life experience box. When you decide to interact and share your writing challenges, it's almost certain that someone in your group will have a solution for you, and you may also provide a solution or tactic for them as well.

How do you feel so far about all of this? I'm sure it's a lot to take in, but just imagine having a conversation one evening about sharing your story with other likeminded individuals. I'm sure it will get you thinking about a few things, which is good. That's the point of it all. Looking back on your life, experiences, lessons, goals, etc., and capturing those moments and talking about them. Collaboration and teamwork is the name of the game. You may even find someone in your group that is a perfect fit to work with on your next project, you never know. No matter which direction you decide to go, I highly encourage you to get the support you need, wherever it may be. Support groups are incredible and life-changing.

So with all of that being said and shared, my question is, what are you waiting for? Let's get started. The Write Your Journey program is here to keep you motivated as you hit your writing goals. I want you to stick to your plan and make it work for you with your level of comfort. This is more than just writing; it's about elevating personally and professionally through your groups and making a phenomenal decision for yourself. Take the time to do your research and choose wisely because at the end of the day it's about your goals and happiness.

For this chapter's exercise, I want you to make a list of ten people who may possibly be an accountability partner for this writing goal of yours. This can include family friends, loved ones, siblings, co-workers, or someone you just met on the same journey. Make a list and reach out to each person to see who would be interested with creating the journey with you.

I want you to remember that you will have full support throughout your writing journey from me; however, you must do your part as well. We are a team, and this is not a one-man show. You hold up your side, and I will hold up my side. Our goal for this chapter is for you to find an accountability partner and share your writing goals with this person. You will share your Write Your Journey template with this special person of your choice, and you will also share your fear or challenge of sharing your story. After completing that, don't forget about sharing the solutions of overcoming that fear or fears around it all. This is easier than you think. Push the excuses to the side, and let's get to work. You have a story to tell the world, and they want to read it like yesterday. Let's go!

*EMBRACE YOUR STORY – WRITE YOUR STORY*
PUBLISH YOUR STORY

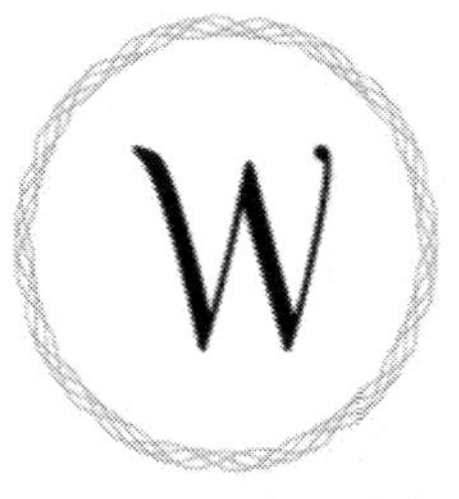


SHARE YOUR STORY WITH SOMEONE TODAY

# Chapter 4
# The Structure of Your Unique Story

Four gold stars for you. You made it to chapter 4. How do you feel? Be honest with yourself, and do not dive into chapter 4 if you haven't completed the assignments from 1, 2, and 3. Now, let's do a quick recap. Did you ever download the Write Your Journey template? Did you complete the template with ten things you love about you, and five memorable life experiences? Did you also write down the reasons why you chose those unique things you love about you?

Out of the five memorable experiences, which one did you decide to write about, and why? Whichever story you chose to write about, you definitely have to dive into your memory bank and think about why this experience was so special to you. Using a travel experience as an example, think about some things you felt surrounding that experience. Where did you travel and who was around? What did you experience? How did it feel, smell, or sound? What about the people you met? How about the food you ate, the places you explored, the restaurants, the open fields, the ocean? What was your experience like? It doesn't matter if you traveled to numerous countries or just one island. The golden question is, did you ever stop to think about how it changed your world? How was it transformational or challenging? With travel stories, it can just be about sharing your unique experience with others. I always tell people that there are so many people out there who are unable to travel and may never even get the opportunity, but your one story and experience can be heard by millions of people. People who aspire to travel but haven't made plans and people who simply cannot travel but wish to live through someone else's stories would appreciate reading yours. In the end though, whatever the reason behind wanting to share that story, just make sure you're confident about sharing it.

If it's not a travel story and it falls in a category of your childhood, family matters, loved ones, or even a relationship, you will still need to think about why you're sharing this story. If you're not comfortable with it, there is no point in reading chapter 4. I want you to be comfortable with where you are, and I want you to be ready for the next level. This is your book, of course, and I don't believe you will let someone borrow it anytime soon, so in the meantime, I want you to take your time through this entire process. You will thank yourself later, and maybe you will thank me too (fingers crossed).

If you're ready to push past the fear of sharing your story, then you are ready to move forward. This simply means you know what story you're writing about and you've already pushed past the fear because you created solutions for those challenges. This also means you worked on your confidence and self-esteem to share your story and you found the perfect accountability partner to work with, which is great. Now let's be honest here: that's a lot to accomplish in a short period of time, so please acknowledge the work that you've done. It's a big deal, and this just means you're focused and serious about your writing goals.

When you feel like you have a story you're comfortable with, the first thing I want you to do for this chapter is this: I want you to email me personally and request your writing template to be emailed to you. Email me at info@denitaaustin.com, with the subject line "writing template request." I will be on standby waiting to hear from you! You will need this writing template by the time you're done reading chapter 4. And guess what: if I receive an email from you then I definitely know you are serious.

Are you ready to get started? In the rest of this chapter you will learn how to create your story structure. At this point you've got the essence of your story, right? You've captured that special moment to write about, and now you must place structure around it. Let's start by thinking about what happened before that special moment you chose to write about. What happened afterward? How did it conclude? This is your beginning, middle, and end of your story that you are sharing with the world. It's a must that you have all three; otherwise, your reader has no point of reference and your story will be a bit confusing for them.

Let me explain in detail with the example below. Your story should be broken down into a few steps in order for you to begin your writing journey. This gives you some order and some key turning points in the story, and makes it easier to keep your thoughts straight and the story moving forward in the right direction as you write. It is the basic structure of your story. Here is an example from one of my stories:

**Part 1 example**: The first time I ever practiced yoga, I honestly felt like a boulder was lifted from my shoulders. I was super anxious yet excited to attend the next session.

**Note:** This is the beginning of the story. Build and elaborate more—go into more detail.

**Part 2 transition example**: So I went to a few yoga studios to learn more about different styles of yoga and the history behind it all. Needless to say I was mesmerized and was considering becoming a yoga teacher. Who would have thought?

**Note:** This is the beginning of the story. Build and elaborate more—go into more detail.

**Part 3 transition example**: I didn't realize how hard it was to become a teacher and the amount of discipline required to complete the certification. It was more of a lifestyle change, which I wasn't prepared for.

**Note:** Build and elaborate more—go into more detail.

**Part 4 transition example**: I had to make the decision to be focused or choose something else to do with my time. I mean, was this something I really wanted to do?

**Note:** Build and elaborate more—go into more detail.

**Part 5 transition example:** In 2004 I became a yoga teacher, and thirteen years later I had the pleasure of teaching at chiropractic offices, universities, and hospitals around the world.

**Note:** Build and elaborate more—go into more detail.

Now it's your turn. Use these examples to structure your story. There are so many different ways to go about this, but I want to provide the easiest way to get started. What are your thoughts on the example given? I encourage you to write this down in your notes simply because I want you to break down your story just like this. As you can see in part one, the topic of discussion is about my experience of yoga and how it made me feel. This gives me an opportunity to elaborate on where the studio was located and what made me participate in the class, who was around me during this time, and what I did after I left the studio. It's super important to give your reader a grand introduction of what you are about to share with them.

In the second part, it goes on to tell you what I did on that journey. I was learning more about different styles of yoga, I spoke about what I was considering. These transitions give me, the storyteller, an opportunity to go into more detail if I choose to. I could share with the reader my thoughts on deciding which yoga school to attend and how I researched the benefits of becoming a yoga teacher. I could also cover all of the little details that are needed to share the story.

By this time, you are creating emotion behind your story, the mood, the setting, and the details of everything. Allow these small steps to unfold naturally into stories. The next example explains more, indicating that I didn't even realize how hard it was to become an instructor and the amount of discipline that was required. So now in this phase of my story I'm in my head with all these thoughts crashing in my brain at once. I'm thinking of new possibilities that I didn't think of previously. The next transition explains the main decision that I had to make and how was I willing to do it.

It might help to think of a major decision you've faced in life? How did it make you feel and who was around with you? Was there anyone around to help you with this transition? How did it make you feel, and what did you think about it? These are the types of golden nuggets you want to think about when you begin your writing journey of sharing your story with the world.

My story then ends with how I became a yoga teacher, and, yes, this is actually a true story. I did become a certified yoga instructor in 2004, and I absolutely love yoga. It's been such an amazing experience in my life and I'm sharing that example with you simply because I want you to be able to break your story down just like that. The who, what, when, where, and then why. I'm not suggesting that the end of your story is a positive one, because everyone's ending is completely different. This is merely an example to get your creative juices flowing for your own unique story you're going to share. Keep in mind that if you need assistance, such as a storytelling coach or mentor, you can always email me at the email address provided in the back of the book. I am always happy to help you get that story out of your head and published. Like I mentioned in chapter 3, the importance of creating your support system is completely your responsibility, so whether you have questions or wish to attend one of our workshops or take one of our courses or even join our ambassador groups, please feel free to do so if it's going to help you on your journey.

You want to structure your story in such a way that it engages readers and helps them relate to you and think of their own lives. During this stage of structuring, if you realize you have the beginning and the middle to your story, but you don't yet have the ending, your story may not be ready to be told. This often happens with very emotional stories where you have not yet worked through the feelings that accompanied the trauma, and therefore you don't really know which way the story ends, because you are really still in the middle of it. This is super important to keep in mind.

Now that you understand how to structure an outline for your book, the homework in this chapter is simply for you to complete the structure of your story by using your writing template that was provided for you by email. As you do this, remember, we all have a story, we just forget how to capture moments in our lives. It doesn't need to be an epic novel; it's your personal story you wish to share with the world for your very own unique reason.

*EMBRACE YOUR STORY – WRITE YOUR STORY*
PUBLISH YOUR STORY

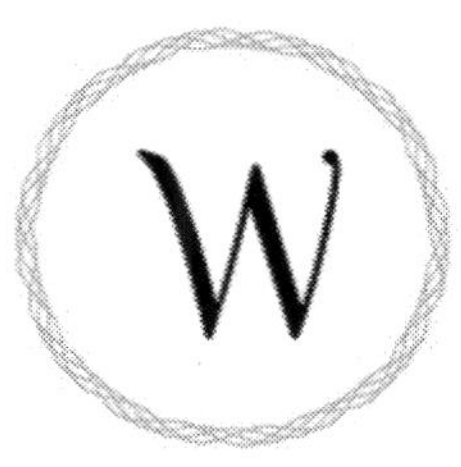

WRITE YOUR JOURNEY

*Life Experiences Published!*

ASK SOMEONE ABOUT THEIR STORY

# Chapter 5
# The Reason Behind Sharing Your Story—The Big Idea

In this chapter, you will reflect on why you want to share your story. The majority of the clients I work with choose to publish their book simply because they want to do it for themselves. They want to commit to something bigger than themselves, and sometimes they want to overcome something emotionally. For them, publishing a book is more of a therapeutic release, to say the least. It could be something they've held onto for years and in order for them to release it from their heart they choose to release it in a published book.

Another reason people want to publish is that seeing your name on the cover of something you can actually touch is something to be proud of. You may fit in the category of someone who wishes to publish a book to earn extra income, or maybe it's something you want to use to save money for a home, car, boat, or even a vacation. Some people wish to become speakers in their industry, and publishing a book will provide leverage for them for reaching their goal. What about publishing a book to build a business and brand around your message? A book could also be an additional product on your website or online store.

Maybe you are trying to pass something down to your family, or you want something to show your kids or grandkids or significant other. Or maybe you are aiming even higher and you want to become rich and famous from your book. Or maybe you wish to inspire other people and transform lives.

No matter what your reason, you hold the key to all of it. It's your vision coming to life with one decision. So the big question is, what is your big idea? What is your special reason behind sharing your story? There's a reason for everything we do, and you must be crystal clear of what your reason is for sharing your story. This helps you create a road map for yourself and get clear on your decision, which will help propel you through to the project's completion. Take your time and really think about it.

While you let that question continue to simmer in your mind, here is a short story for you. A close friend of mine recently created a blog. She just wanted to share her random excursions, traveling and meeting people along the way, with people around the world. She also wanted to share how she was able to do it on a budget. Since she is an artist, it can be a bit challenging to create a comfortable lifestyle, and even more so if you want to travel the world. But that is exactly what she is doing—being a super-amazing artist who travels the world on a budget selling her art and meeting as many people as she can. Now, this story may apply mostly to bloggers reading this book, but I thought it would be a great example to share.

Although she is super passionate about her blog and she shares weekly tips while she travels, we decided to sit down and chat about her goals for the blog and how the blog would be able to help her earn a living while she's traveling. These are conversations that I can have for hours. I absolutely love talking to creative people. There is something about thinking outside the box that allows us to push beyond limitations. So after an hour into our girl time, I asked her if she had ever considered writing a book. Her first response to me was, "About what? What would I write about? Who would read it, and how do I even get started?" Then she ended her long statement and said, "I don't think anyone would be interested with my story." Bingo! I knew right then and there that this conversation would last a few hours—but don't worry, I won't bore you with all the details. However, I will share with you how this conversation unfolded. I was able to explain to her that it would be beneficial for her to write about her personal story. Meaning, who is she, what her background is, where she came from, and how she even came up with the idea of creating a blog. Now, of course, she could also share her journey of getting started with writing her blog and what that entails or how she became an artist and what pitfalls to avoid on your journey of becoming an artist. This particular story will inspire other individuals who may want to start a blog or become an artist or traveler. By her sharing her story, it would also give her audience a peek behind the scenes of who she is besides the articles she writes on her blog and the pictures she posts. Another bonus from all of this is simply the obvious. You could literally take this example of her writing and publishing her story in so many different directions. However, I explained to her that her book would provide extra income for her while she's a traveling artist. When I explained that to her, her eyes lit up. It was as if a spark went off in her brain. She realized that she could earn a living for herself while traveling, just by sharing her personal experiences in life that will inspire others. "Sounds like a plan to me," she said. This is what I inspire you to do for your story, of course, but first, think about your reason behind it all.

So it's homework time! Yes, homework ☺. Now that you've had a little time to think about why you are writing your story, write down three main reasons for you writing and publishing your book. Then I want you to write down the ideal outcome from doing so. As a friendly reminder, if you need a sounding board, I'm just an email away.

*EMBRACE YOUR STORY – WRITE YOUR STORY*
PUBLISH YOUR STORY

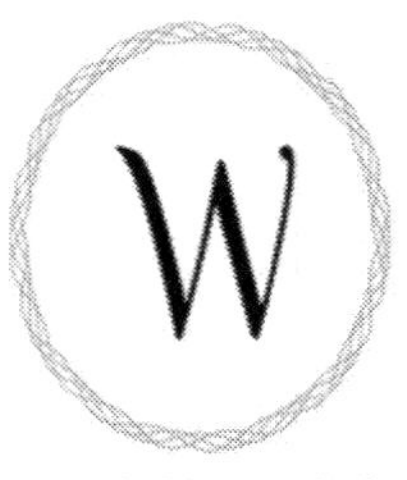

WRITE YOUR JOURNEY

*Life Experiences Published!*

PLACE YOUR STAMP ON THE WORLD
BY SHARING YOUR STORY

# Chapter 6
# The Journey in a Journal

It's all about the journey. Every single time you leave your home, record your experiences. It doesn't matter how you choose to document them—in a notebook, on a blog, or with a writing app—find a way that fits your personality and lifestyle. Embrace it and dive in. You can capture moments while you're driving by recording your voice. Maybe you could take photographs to possibly create a photography book later on to share at your dinner party. You know what you enjoy doing and what makes you happy, so surround yourself with that. Do an activity that brings joy to your life, and document it. We are surrounded by so much inspiration, but we are distracted by the obvious.

## 3 GOLDEN REASONS TO KEEP A JOURNAL

- Our journal is our story.
- As we write our journey, we find accountability to ourselves.
- Writing causes us to become more intentional in any pursuit—and to find inspiration beyond the obvious places right in front of us.

## 3 QUESTIONS FOR YOU (Write Your Answers Below)

1. How are you documenting special moments in your life? Camera, recording, writing or just verbal?
2. When was the last time you documented a transformational experience in your life?
3. What inspires you to write?

______________________________________________

______________________________________________

______________________________________________

______________________________________________

______________________________________________

______________________________________________

Write for yourself, not for others. As you do, write with the truest goal of putting onto paper your thoughts and actions. It's super easy to get caught up in spelling and grammar, and, yes, although this is important, it's not important in the beginning stages of getting your story out of your head and onto paper. There will be days when you'll be motivated to write, and others days when you're not. Don't be motivated by how much you write. Focus on substance and the vivid details of a story. Every single time I decide to go off on one of my excursions, I usually capture moments using this easy three-step technique:

1. Create a video or take a photo of my exact location.
2. Record my voice to capture what I'm experiencing in that very moment.
3. Write down a note in my journal of my surroundings, thoughts, etc.

When I return to my writing studio, I am able to relive that moment to begin my writing journey. I'm able to watch the video as many times as I please or gaze at the inspiring photo that was taken. This allows me to elaborate on that special moment to dig deeper. When I listen to my voice, I can literally add the emotion behind it all to compliment the scenery and atmosphere. Taking notes, recording my voice, and simply taking a few photos make all the difference in remembering an experience you'll never get back.

That's why I encourage you to capture each moment that's special to you. I've done this quite a few times while hiking. It was the best decision ever.

Your story is important and is meant to be shared. You may not realize it, but there are millions of people who need to read your story. Why? Maybe for inspiration or comfort, or maybe it will let them know they're not alone. But you can't tell it unless you can remember it well!

Now it's time for more homework! Woo-hoo!

1. I highly recommend that you **purchase a journal** to document your life experiences or to visit memory lane on past experiences you wish to share with the world.
2. **Find an accountability partner to work with** you on your writing journey. Maybe you both can create magic together, which may lead to a future writing project.
3. **Download your WYJ contract** to yourself. Remember to take full responsibility for your happiness and your goals. www.DenitaAustin.com/Committmenttoselfcontract

*EMBRACE YOUR STORY – WRITE YOUR STORY*
PUBLISH YOUR STORY

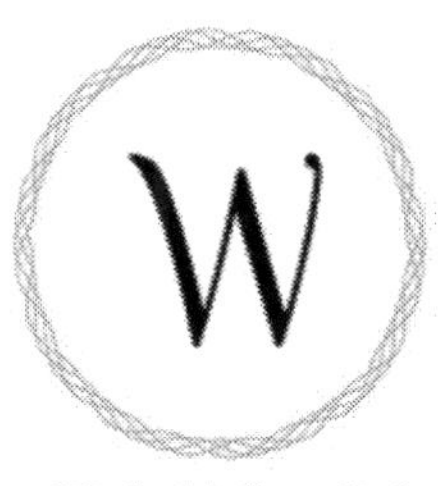


WRITE YOUR JOURNEY

*Life Experiences Published!*

THE WORLD IS WAITING ON YOUR STORY

# Chapter 7
# The Power of Storytelling

We tell stories every single day and don't even realize it. I mean, let's think about this for a moment. We have discussions on how we see the past, how we envision the future or hope for the future to unfold, and how we create visions in our minds to manifest in the present. All of these are stories. If you are an entrepreneur, have you ever thought about how you convey a message about your brand, product, or service? These are stories as well. *Stories emotionalize information.* Did you catch that? *"A story gives color and depth to otherwise bland material, and it allows people to connect with the message in a deeper, more meaningful way."* I love a good story that has passion and authenticity behind it. I mean, let's face it, have you ever sat with a few friends and someone shared a story but for some reason you were asleep with your eyes wide open because you were bored to death? I'm sure you were bored simply because the story had no color or depth, not to mention no emotion or passion.

So what is my point? Never underestimate the power of your story. Be proud of your past and the present chapter of your life. Share your story with integrity, truth, and raw emotion. The power of storytelling is life changing, and it gives you an opportunity to challenge the story you're currently living. Our experiences create our present situations and our future. Once you hear yourself share your personal story out loud, it feels as though you are placing a mirror right in front of your face. This is why I speak so passionately about Writing Your Journey program. Not only are you tapping into your personal story vault, but you are also embarking on something bigger than yourself. It forces you to dig deeper to create the story you wish to live. What chapter are you currently living? And are you ready to write the next chapter of your life?

I have one more story to share with you before completing this book. Are you ready? I sure hope so. Grab another cup of coffee or your favorite beverage for this one. You will need it (smile).

When I was a young child, I used to literally stare at my grandmother as if she was from another planet. There was something different about her, but I couldn't put my finger on it. It was the way she viewed the world and the way she cooked her food and the way she looked. Her values were quite unique, and I just couldn't find a way to connect with her; I just did what I was told. I didn't spend that much time with her, but I did spend enough time to know something was uniquely different about her. I was curious to know why she looked the way she did, and I felt like we were from two different worlds. My grandmother, who is still living now, by the way, is one of eight siblings. Her brothers and her sisters all look alike as if they are all twins, and of course, growing up, I stared at them as well. It was like, why do you look so different from me, and where did you come from? So let's talk about features. My grandmother is five foot four with long black hair that damn near swept the floor when I was growing up. She has distinctive facial features, as her eyes are tight and slanted, with olive skin and a round face. She would always wear her hair in a long braid that could literally be a jump rope. She never really said much, but said a lot at the same time. I always wanted to just sit with her and inquire about her upbringing and what life was like when she was a child. I wanted to know what was school like for her and about her parents. I had so many questions. It took me thirty-seven years to realize that my family has a lot of history no one knows about. My grandmother is pure Native American from a tribe called Blackfoot. When I found this out, I was completely blown away and didn't know what to do with this information. I felt like my eyes were now open to life from a different perspective. And I couldn't believe after all these years, I was just now retrieving this information. How would you feel in this situation? Do you know your family heritage? Do you know the history of your family and who holds the key to this information? This is the beginning of a new journey for me, and I'm honestly pretty excited about it.

Why do I share this with you? you ask. Simply because here we have another story yet to be told, but at the same time it also opens up a door for you to share your family history and story. It also gives you something to think about. We are full of stories, but as we get older and older the stories become dust and we forget about them or decide to bury them to never be told. As you're reading this book and another personal story of mine, I've decided to go on this quest to learn more about my family history, and I plan to share the details with you in the next chapter of my life.

Your last homework assignment!

1. Find out who holds the golden key to your family story and heritage. This will be quite the conversation during the holidays.
2. If you could share any story about your life with the world, what would it be and why?

*EMBRACE YOUR STORY – WRITE YOUR STORY*
PUBLISH YOUR STORY

NAME ONE OF YOUR WRITING CHALLENGES

# Chapter 8
# Message from the Author

I want to take this opportunity to thank you for reading this book. My goal was to inspire and motivate you to move forward on your writing journey. I hope you are ready by now to dive into your memory bank, write that story, and prepare it to get published. Place your stamp in the world and create a legacy. The question will never be why. The question is, why not? We only live once, so live your best life. Show up, give, and be your best!

I encourage you to share your story with the world. It's the most refreshing and rewarding thing I've ever done. It completely changed my world. Not only did it build confidence within me, but it also created a platform upon which I could reach higher, not afraid of living life on my terms. I've learned so much on this writing journey, and I'm still learning. Everything I've learned so far I'm eager to share with you, and this is why I wrote this book for you to read. I hope you enjoyed it!

I also want to encourage you to keep writing. After you release one story into the world, don't stop there. Keep going! Your life and your world doesn't revolve around one story and one experience. There are plenty of stories I know you have to share that will truly inspire others.

Your story is your legacy, life experiences and lessons. It's your contribution to the world. By sharing your story, you are inspiring others to do the same. By doing this, you are creating a community around what you have experienced in your life, and you will be surprised with whom you may connect with.

I have more stories to share with you too, but I will save those stories for when we meet face-to-face. The next time you're in LA, let's meet for coffee. This time next year, who will you be? What is your Story now and what will it be next year?

*EMBRACE YOUR STORY – WRITE YOUR STORY*: PUBLISH YOUR STORY

SHARE YOUR STORY AT MY NEXT EVENT

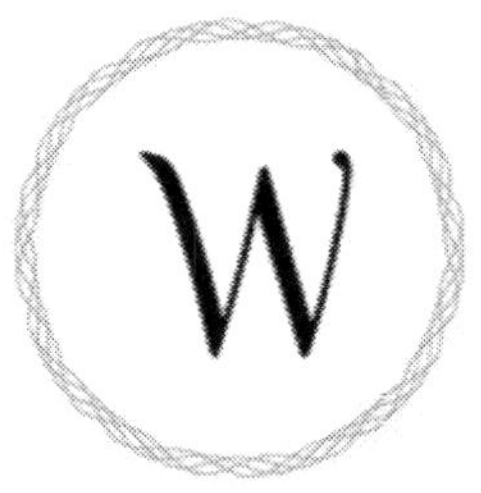

WRITE YOUR JOURNEY

*Life Experiences Published!*

Need Help Writing And Publishing Your Story? Check out my Online Course and workshops @ Denitaaustin.com

Currently looking for a storytelling mentor or coach? Send me a quick email to set up a chat to discuss your story at info@denitaaustin.com to be published

If you are not quite ready to write an entire book on your own, but still wish to share your story, we have quite a few co-author opportunities that may work for you.

You can learn more @ DenitaAustin.com/coauthor

STAY IN TOUCH

DENITAAUSTIN.COM

info@denitaaustin.com

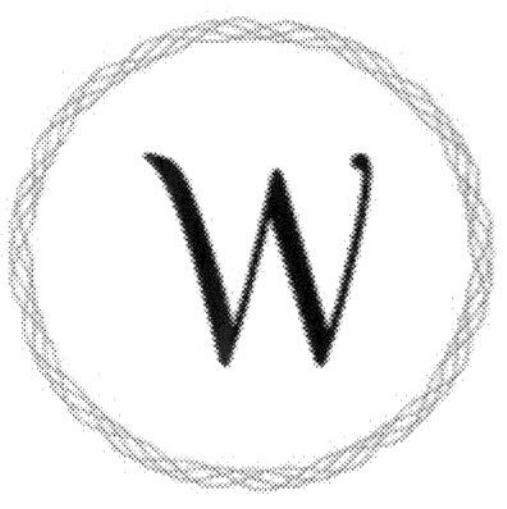

WRITE YOUR JOURNEY

*Life Experiences Published!*

Made in the USA
Middletown, DE
06 March 2020

85962507R00040